# Sewers and Gutters

### Sharon Katz Cooper

Chicago, Illinois

W9-ALW-721

**www.heinemannraintree.com**
Visit our website to find out more information about Heinemann-Raintree books.

**To order:**
☎ Phone 888-454-2279
💻 Visit www.heinemannraintree.com to browse our catalog and order online.

© 2010 Raintree
an imprint of Capstone Global Library, LLC
Chicago, Illinois

Edited by Charlotte Guillain, Rebecca Rissman, and Sian Smith
Designed by Joanna Hinton-Malivoire
Picture research by Tracy Cummins and Heather Mauldin
Originated by Chroma Graphics (Overseas) Pte. Ltd
Printed and bound in China by Leo Paper Products

14 13 12 11 10
10 9 8 7 6 5 4 3 2 1

**Library of Congress Cataloging-in-Publication Data**
Katz Cooper, Sharon.
Sewers and gutters / Sharon Katz Cooper.
p. cm. -- (Horrible habitats)
Includes bibliographical references and index. ISBN 978-1-4109-3490-1 (hc)
ISBN 978-1-4109-3498-7 (pb)
1. Urban ecology (Biology)--Juvenile literature. 2. Urban pests--Habitat--Juvenile literature. 3. Sewerage--Juvenile literature. 4. Street gutters--Juvenile literature.
I. Title.
QH541.5.C6K3825 2009
577.5'6--dc22
                    2009002592

**Acknowledgments**
The author and publisher are grateful to the following for permission to reproduce copyright material: Age Fotostock p. **16** (© Bildagentur Waldhaeusl/waldhaeusl com); Alamy pp. **4** (© Arco Images GmbH), **7** (© Mike Rinnan), **11** (© Mike Lane), **26** (© Ashley Cooper); Animals Animals p. **13** (© Mickey Gibson); Ardea p. **8** (© John Daniels); DRK Photo p. **29** (© William P. Leonard); Dwight Kuhn Photography pp. **14**, **15** (© Dave Kuhn); Getty Images pp. **5** (© Bert Klassen), **19** (© Joe Raedle/Staff); Minden p. **10** (© Stephen Dalton); National Geographic Stock p. **9** (© James L. Stanfield); Nature Picture Library pp. **20** (© Phil Savoie), **23** (© Jane Burton); Photolibrary pp. **6** (© Photononstop/Jacques Loic), **12** (© Bartomeu Borrell), **24** (© Mike Anich); Photo Researchers, Inc. p. **21** (© Dr. Merlin D. Tuttle/Bat Conservation International); Shutterstock pp. **17** (© Mau Horng), **18** (© Saniphoto), **22** (© Christopher Tan Teck Hean), **25** (© Steve McWilliam), **27** (© Timothy Large).

Cover photograph of a rat reproduced with permission of Ardea (© John Daniels].

Some words are shown in bold, **like this**. You can find out what they mean by looking in the glossary.

# Contents

# What Is a Habitat?

A **habitat** is a place where plants and animals can find what they need to live. What are those needs? Plants and animals need food, water, and shelter.

rat →

5

Almost any place can be a **habitat**. You can find **sewers** under the streets. Sewers are filled with the dirty water from streets, houses, and toilets.

this way to the sewer

What could you find living in the dirty water and rotting leaves in this gutter?

A **gutter** is the tube that catches leaves and water from the roofs of houses. Even sewers and gutters are habitats!

# Rats all Around

Rats live everywhere people do. There are thousands and even millions of them in city **sewers**. Why? They can find lots of water and food down there.

Norway rat

These hungry rats are searching for food.

nest

Rats often build their nests in places connected to **sewers**. They go into the sewer to find food.

11

# Roach Restaurants

Roaches are easy to find in **sewers**. They feed on dead and rotting plants and animals. That is exactly what they find down there. They also like to be in the dark, and it is always dark in the sewers!

These roaches are enjoying rotting kiwi fruit.

Cockroaches need to drink. They sometimes get water from toilets and dirty puddles. This is one reason they spread dirt and carry **diseases**.

Lots of poo can be found in sewers. This cockroach is eating some!

poo ➜

Roaches are insects. They have six legs and run very fast. They leave behind a trail of smelly, oily liquid. Other roaches like the smell and come running.

legs

17

# Sewer Surprises

Some people have unkindly flushed baby alligators down the toilet in the past. Anything that is flushed down a toilet travels to the **sewers**.

baby alligator

## FUN FACT

Alligators have been found in sewers. Young alligators might be able to live in a sewer for a while by eating rats. It is unlikely that any fully grown alligators could be found in sewers today, though.

19

# Big Brown Bats

Brown bats sometimes sleep for the winter in **sewers** and other dark underground places. This is called **hibernation**. They even sleep in graveyards.

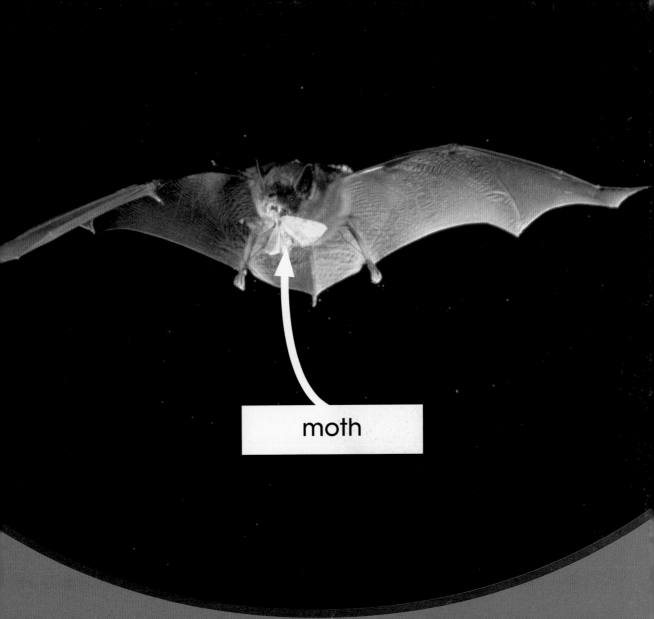

moth

**FUN FACT**

Brown bats fly out at night
to look for insects to eat.
They eat mosquitoes,
beetles, and moths.

# Slimy Snails and Slugs

You may find snails moving slowly around **gutters**. Snails' bodies make a lot of slime. This slime is so thick that it acts like a suction cup. The suction helps snails move upside down!

## FUN FACT

Snails move by creeping along on a flat foot underneath their bodies. Unlike us, snails only have one foot!

## FUN FACT

Snails can't hear but they can feel vibrations.

**Gutters** also attract slugs. This is because slugs like to eat rotting plants and leaves. Just like snails, slugs are covered with a slime called **mucus**. Mucus keeps their skins **moist**, or lightly wet.

## FUN FACT

Slug bodies are often covered with mites. Mites are tiny creatures that will bite into a slug's skin and suck its blood.

Slugs trail slime from their undersides. This slime helps them slide along the ground. They leave a trail of slime behind them.

slug trail

26

## FUN FACT

Slugs have holes in the sides of their bodies! A slug takes air into its body through this hole and the hole can open or close.

27

# Follow a Slug

**What you need:**
- your eyes
- an area where you can find slugs

**What to do:**
1. Go outside after it has rained and look around.

2. Find a slug and look for its slime trail.

3. How far back can you trace it? Can you see where it has been? Where do you think it might be going? Can you see the hole in the slug's side?

29

# Glossary

**disease**  illness

**gutter**  tube that catches water from the roofs of houses. Many rotting leaves get stuck in gutters, too.

**habitat**  place where plants and animals live and grow

**hibernation**  sleeping for a long time in winter, saving energy

**moist**  slightly wet or damp

**mucus**  slippery stuff that animals produce from their bodies

**sewer**  place under the street where the dirty water from streets and houses goes

# Find Out More

**Find out**

Which snails are the fastest?

## Books to Read

Dickmann, Nancy. *Cockroaches.* Chicago: Raintree, 2005.

Llewellyn, Claire. *Snails and Slugs.* New York: Children's Press, 2002.

Marrin, Albert. *Oh Rats! The Story of Rats and People.* New York: Dutton Juvenile, 2006.

## Websites

**http:// www.pestworldforkids.org/rats.html**
Find out about different kinds of rats on this Website.

**http://www.geocities.com/sseagraves/allaboutsnails.htm**
This Website is packed with snail facts and activities.

**http://www.sciencenewsforkids.org/articles/20070808/Feature1.asp**
Learn about how slime helps snails and slugs move around.

**http://yucky.discovery.com/flash/roaches/**
You can learn all about roaches here.

# Index